GOD'S RHYTHM OF LIFE

D1257487

SEASONS OF THE LORD

UNDERSTANDING THE JEWISH ROOTS OF THE CHURCH

WILLIAM J. MORFORD

Published by Shalom Ministries, Inc.

© 2004 Rev. William J. Morford
301 Creek Side Lane
Lexington, SC 29072
803-808-5275
Email: wjm@thepowernewtestament.com
Website: www.thepowernewtestament.com

ISBN 0-9664523-3-X

DEDICATION

God's Rhythm of Life is dedicated to my wife, Jeanie, who has encouraged me to write this and to finally have it published. A project of this nature requires a great deal of research, then writing and rewriting to have something meaningful. Jeanie is an astute proofreader as well as an encourager.

CONTENTS

GOD'S RHYTHM OF LIFE

UNDERSTANDING THE JEWISH ROOTS OF THE CHURCH..You do not support the root, but the root supports you. Romans 11:18

THE SEASONS OF THE LORD
OFTEN REFERRED TO AS *THE FEASTS OF ISRAEL*

INTRODUCTION

God's Rhythm of Life is about the Jewishness of Jesus and of our Scriptures. Isaiah prophesied about Christians coming into Jewish Roots when he wrote **This one will say: 'I am the Lord God's,' and the other one will call [himself] by the name of Jacob; this one will sign his allegiance to the Lord God, and adopt the name of Israel.** (Isaiah 44:5 Artscroll Tanakh)

Remember the Torah of Moses my servant, which I commanded him in Horeb for all Israel, with the statutes and judgments. (Malachi 3:22) **Jesus said: "Do not think that I came to annul, to bring an**

incorrect interpretation to, the Torah or the Prophets: I did not come to annul but to bring *spiritual* abundance, for the Torah to be obeyed as it should be and God's promises to receive fulfillment. 18. For truly I say to you: until the sky and the Earth would pass away, not one yod or one vav could ever pass away from the Torah, until everything would come to pass. (Matthew 5:17,18)

God's Rhythm of Life tells of many Jewish customs, but the goal of this book is to bring Christians into an appreciation of the Jewish heritage and what all the authors of the New Testament believed. A number of Jewish traditions are mentioned, but Christians are not to copy those traditions. We are to return to Torah, the Scriptures of the authors of the New Testament.

Paul tells us we are grafted in to the Jewish, domestic, olive tree (Romans 11:17). As in the natural, a branch grafted in does not produce the domestic olive, but the wild olive of its nature. The advantage of the graft is that the strength of the root is added to the grafted branch, to produce stronger fruit. Christians are not to produce copies of the fruit of Rabbinic Judaism, but a new fruit of Torah-believing, Scripture-based worshippers of the Most High God. The separation from our Jewish roots was a deliberate act by the early Church to erase the Jewish roots, including God's appointed seasons. That separation hinders our relationship with our Heavenly Father. In another analogy Jesus said,

14. I AM the Good Shepherd and I know My *sheep* and My *sheep* know Me, 15. just as the Father knows Me and I know the Father, and I lay down My life on behalf of the sheep. 16. But I also have sheep that are not from this sheepfold: and it is necessary for Me to lead those and they will hear My voice, and they will become one flock, one Shepherd. (John 10:14-16. See Ezekiel 34:23, 37:24)

We are to study the Jewish traditions and glean the spiritual meanings, because many of those traditions are anointed and give beautiful insight. Then we are to focus on the Scriptural basis for each tradition, and be led by Scripture to bring change in the way we worship and celebrate the Seasons of the Lord. Paul admonished the Corinthians in his first letter to them,

4:6. **And these things, brothers, by what I have said of myself and Apollos I have shown you what applies to all Christian teachers, so that you would learn through us 'Not *to go* beyond what has been written, *Scripture*,' so that you would not be proud on behalf of the one against another.** We are to go to what Paul called Scripture, the Jewish Tanakh, which Christians call Old Testament.

Understanding the Jewishness of Jesus and the Jewish customs in the New Testament brings light to many hidden truths in the New Testament and brings us closer to God's truth. The goal of this series is to draw Christians into a desire to study about their Jewish roots and to begin to follow the Biblical call to do the things presented in Scripture. Jesus honored the Seasons outlined in this booklet. Should we do less?

Throughout God's Rhythm of Life there are two terms we need to understand, Torah and Tanakh. The Torah refers specifically to the first five books of the Bible. Prophets includes the books of Joshua, Judges, Samuel, Kings, and Isaiah through Malachi except for Daniel. In the New Testament the term Torah and Prophets often refers to the entire Hebrew Scriptures (Tanakh), which Christians call Old Testament. In most of our translations Torah is translated Law, but Law is **not** appropriate because it has caused Christians to think that the Old Testament is a rigid, authoritarian book that no longer has much application to our lives. Torah is the correct term because in Hebrew Torah means teaching or instruction. It is the Lord's instruction concerning relationships with other human beings and with Him. Throughout Scripture whenever you read **law**, you should automatically change **law** to **Torah**, remembering that Torah means teaching or instruction. There are a few cases in Romans, Galatians, and Colossians when Paul was writing about legalism that **law** is appropriate, about twenty times in all. Those are the only exceptions, so please change **law** to **Torah**, or just read The Power New Testament. (See the back cover re: The Power New Testament.)

Jesus was born to Jewish parents and was brought up keeping the commandments of the Tanakh, which is called Old Testament by Christians. His Jewishness is readily apparent because, after the birth of Jesus, Mary and Joseph immediately followed all the commandments regarding circumcision, purification, and dedication. He was circumcised at eight days old as recorded in Luke 2:21. **And when *the* eight days were completed to circumcise Him His name was called Jesus, being called that by the angel to the one who conceived Him in her womb.** At thirty-three days He was dedicated; that is, offered and redeemed at the temple. This was ordered in Exodus 13:2, 12, 13, & 15.

13:2. **Sanctify to me all the firstborn, whatever opens the womb among the people of Israel, both of man and of beast; it is mine.**

13:12. **That you shall set apart to the Lord all that**

opens the matrix, and every firstling that comes of a beast which you have; the males shall be the Lord's.

13:13. .. and all the firstborn of man among your children shall you redeem.

13:15. And it came to pass, when Pharaoh would hardly let us go, that the Lord slew all the firstborn in the land of Egypt, both the firstborn of man, and the firstborn of beast; therefore I sacrifice to the Lord all that opens the matrix, being males; but all the firstborn of my children I redeem.

For the mother's purification we have ; **Speak to the people of Israel, saying, If a woman conceives, and bears a male child; then she shall be unclean seven days; as in the days of her menstruation, shall she be unclean. 3. And in the eighth day the flesh of his foreskin shall be circumcised. 4. And she shall then continue in the blood of her purifying for thirty-three days; she shall touch no consecrated thing, nor come into the sanctuary, until the days of her purifying be fulfilled.** (Leviticus 12:2-4) Mary's purification was recorded in Luke 2:22. **And when the days of their purification were completed according to the Torah of Moses, they brought Him up to Jerusalem to present *Him* to the Lord, 23. just as it has been written in *the* Torah of *the* Lord that every male opening the womb will be called holy to the Lord.** Mary's purification and Jesus' dedication, that is His offering and redemption, were made simultaneously as ordered in those verses.

Joseph and Mary attended the feasts in Jerusalem regularly. As Jesus matured, He was accepted into adulthood with a service that later came to be called Bar Mitzvah, reported in Luke 2:41-47. 41. **And His parents were going to Jerusalem from year to year to the Feast of Passover. 42. And when He was twelve years *old*, they went up for the feast according to *their* custom *and for His Bar Mitzvah* (coming of age) 43. and when the days were completed, on their return the child Jesus remained in Jerusalem, but His parents did not know *that*. 44. And thinking He was in the caravan they came a day *on the* way and**

they were searching *for* Him among their relatives and acquaintances, 45. but when they did not find Him they returned to Jerusalem looking for Him. 46. Then it happened after three days they found Him in the temple, sitting in the middle of the teachers and listening to them and questioning them: 47. and all those who heard Him were amazed over His understanding and answers. This is speaking of the ceremony that today is called Bar Mitzvah. While not called that in Jesus' day, He went through a ceremony similar to today's Bar Mitzvah to give evidence of His knowledge and that He was now to be considered an adult.

His being considered an adult after that ceremony was the reason He was not missed by Mary and Joseph on the first day of their return home. To travel between Jerusalem and cities more than an hour or two away the people would walk in large groups, with the men at the ends for protection and the women and children in the middle. On the way to Jerusalem Jesus traveled with the women and children, but on the return Mary would

have expected Him to walk with the men and Joseph
assumed He was with the group of men at the other end.

At the beginning of His ministry Jesus was baptized,
immersed, in the Jordan River. The Greek word
Baptisma means Immersion and the Jewish people had
been immersing themselves for purification for many
generations before the birth of Jesus. Baptism for
purification was made after someone was defiled, such
as by a corpse or blood, or when someone who had not
been worshipping repented and returned to the Lord.
Those who were repenting were the ones that were
called by John and later by Jesus, Who said in Matthew
4:17 .. **You must continually repent: for the kingdom
of the heavens has come near.**

Jesus continued to go to Jerusalem to celebrate
feasts during His ministry, with the Gospel of John
recording attendance at more feasts than any other
Gospel. The number of feasts named in John gives us
the chronology, so we know that He ministered for three
and a half years. Passover is mentioned at three
distinctly different times, Sukkot (Tabernacles) and

Hanukkah are mentioned and an unnamed feast in John 5:1 could be Shavuot, commonly called Pentecost by Christians, although some believe John 5:1 to be another Passover.

THE FEASTS IN JOHN ARE:

2:13 **And the Passover of the Jewish people was drawing near, and Jesus went up to Jerusalem.** (Attendance at Passovers is also recorded in Chapters. 12 & 13.)

5:1. **After these things there was a feast of the Jewish people and Jesus went up to Jerusalem.**

7:2 & 14. 2. **And the Feast of Booths of the Jewish people was near.** 14. **And now, in the middle of the feast, Jesus went up to the temple and He was teaching.**

10:22. **At that time it was the Feast of Dedication for those in Jerusalem. It was winter,** 23. **and Jesus was walking in the temple, on Solomon's Porch.** The Hebrew name for this feast is "Hanukkah." There are numerous additional references to His attending feasts throughout the Gospels.

Jesus taught that every letter of the Jewish Scriptures was important. Matthew 5:17. **Do not think that I came to abolish the Torah or the Prophets: I did not come to abolish but to bring *spiritual* abundance.** 18. **For truly I say to you: until the sky and the earth would pass away, not one yod or one vav could ever pass away from the Torah, until everything would come to pass.** The word translated yod is iota, the Greek equivalent of the Hebrew letter yod, the smallest letter of the Hebrew alphabet. The word translated vav is more involved because there is no "v" sound in the Greek language. To express the letter "v" in Greek, both Matthew and Luke (Luke 16:17) used the word keraia, which means small horn or hook. The word vav in Hebrew is more than just the name of a letter. It is a word that means hook, so Matthew and Luke used keraia to indicate that Jesus referred to the vav, which is the second smallest letter in the Hebrew alphabet. Not only are the yod and vav the two smallest letters in Hebrew, but they are also called soft letters because they can at times be left out of a word and the word would not be misspelled. Jesus was thus saying that even the letters that can legitimately be left out of a word would not be left out of the Torah or the Prophets.

Jesus criticized the Pharisees for certain interpretations of Scripture. In Matthew 23:23 He criticized them because even though they were tithing herbs often grown in very small gardens, even just flower pots, they were missing the higher things on which we are to focus. Another name for this attention to minor details is legalism, which is still alive today in our churches, with requirements of different kinds, whether hairstyles, dress codes, rules on divorce, the dance, praise and worship, and on and on.

SEASONS

The Church is being called to understand its Jewish roots while it prepares for the return of its Jewish Messiah. Something that is profitable is the study and honoring of the Seasons of the Lord. The Seasons are referred to as the **Rhythm of Life** by the Jewish people, as they bring a cycle of thanksgiving to God, offerings, repentance, and celebration: emotions from remorse to extreme joy. These are sometimes referred to as the Feasts of Israel, but when they are listed in Leviticus 23 they are called the Seasons of the Lord. They focus on the seasons we are to honor throughout the year. These seasons form the framework of Godly living that is to become a pattern for us, going from repentance to joy with celebrations and a passion for life. Leviticus 23:1. **And the Lord spoke to Moses, saying,** 2. **Speak to the people of Israel, and say to them, 'The seasons of the Lord, which you shall proclaim to be holy gatherings, these are My seasons.'**

SABBATH

Hebrew Name: Shabbat

Time: Every Friday at sundown until Saturday at
sundown.

Symbolized by two candlesticks and a loaf of hallah bread, both symbols taken from the dining room table because the Sabbath worship takes place mainly in the home.

The first of the seasons in Leviticus 23 is the Sabbath. Verse 3. **Six days shall work be done; but the seventh day is the Sabbath of rest, a holy gathering; you shall do no work in it; it is the Sabbath of the Lord in all your dwellings.** On the weekly Sabbath we are to do no work at all, plus additional proscriptions that are discussed in the following paragraphs. There are partial Sabbaths on certain of the Seasons on which light work is permitted, but not going in to regular employment.

The activities forbidden on the weekly Sabbath and Yom Kippur are:

Do not work. Exodus 20:8. **Remember the Sabbath day, to keep it holy. 9. Six days shall you labor, and do all your work;** 10. **But the seventh day is the Sabbath of the Lord your God; in it you shall not do any manner of work, you, nor your son, nor your daughter, your manservant, nor your maidservant, nor your cattle, nor your stranger that is within your gates;** 11. **For in six days the Lord made heaven and earth, the sea, and all that is in them, and rested the seventh day; therefore the Lord blessed the Sabbath day, and made it holy.** We are not even to put our animals to work on the Sabbath. Servants are not to work. However, from Jesus' statements about caring for children and domestic animals we know that not only He, but also the Pharisees approved of necessary care of people and animals. Jesus said, **Then He said to**

4

them, "A son or ox of any of you will fall into a well, and will any *of you* not immediately pull him up on a Sabbath day? (Luke 14:5) Hospital care and other emergency services are to be performed on the Sabbath.

Do not travel. Exodus 19:29. **See, because the Lord has given you the Sabbath, therefore he gives you on the sixth day the bread of two days; abide you every man in his place, let no man go out of his place on the seventh day.** This means to stay close to home, but does not specify any distance. Basically, it means not to go out of town, not to use the Sabbath as a day of travel.

Do not cook. Exodus 35:3. **You shall kindle no fire throughout your habitations upon the Sabbath day.** This has been taken as a command not to cook, which means that the wife gets to spend the time with her family, not cooking and cleaning up the kitchen all Sabbath afternoon.

5

Do not carry a large load. Jeremiah 17:21. **Thus says the Lord; Take heed to yourselves, and bear no burden on the Sabbath day, nor bring it in by the gates of Jerusalem; 22. Do not carry a burden out of your houses on the Sabbath day, nor do you any work, but sanctify the Sabbath day, as I commanded your fathers.** This is self-explanatory, not to carry large loads on the Sabbath.

Do not sell or buy. Nehemiah 10:32. **And if the peoples of the land bring ware or any grain on the Sabbath day to sell, we will not buy it from them on the Sabbath, or on a holy day; and we will forego the crops of the seventh year, and the exaction of every debt.**

Nehemiah 13:15. **In those days I saw in Judah men treading wine presses on the Sabbath, and bringing in sheaves, and loading them on donkeys; and also wine, grapes, and figs, and all kinds of burdens, which they brought into Jerusalem on the Sabbath day; and I warned them on the day when they sold**

**food. 16. Men of Tyre, who lived there, brought fish,
and all kinds of ware, and sold on the Sabbath to the
people of Judah, and in Jerusalem. 17. Then I
confronted the nobles of Judah, and said to them,
What evil thing is this that you are doing, profaning
the Sabbath day? 18. Did not your fathers act this
way, and did not our God bring all this evil upon us,
and upon this city? Yet you bring more wrath upon
Israel by profaning the Sabbath.** These two passages
are related to the Jeremiah passage not to bear a
burden. The purpose of most burdens was for either
buying or selling, both of which are forbidden here.
Because of this, money is neither carried nor discussed
on the Sabbath by Orthodox Jewish people. Even if not
related to buying and selling, bearing burdens is still
forbidden.

What constitutes a burden is not defined in Scripture,
but Jesus gave an idea about what is acceptable when
He ordered a man to carry his pallet in John 5:8. **Jesus
said to him, "You must immediately get up, you**

must at once take your pallet and you must continually walk." 9. And immediately the man became well and he took his pallet and he was walking. But it was a Sabbath on that day. 10. Therefore the Jewish people were saying to the one who had been healed, "It is *the* Sabbath, and it is not permitted for you to take your pallet."

Other things Jesus did on the Sabbath were not forbidden by Scripture, but by the legalistic definitions of the Pharisees. Healing is definitely permitted. Traveling short distances, as when the disciples were going through a grain field was not criticized even by the Pharisees. Their criticism was for picking a few heads of grain, which is not forbidden in Scripture. A farmer could not harvest on the Sabbath, and a family could not gather an entire meal, but a snack was not forbidden.

The purpose of the Sabbath is to rest with the Lord, as God rested on the seventh day. All members of the family are to spend this time together so everyone in the household is to stay close to home, doing no manner of work or busying with the computer or anything else. It is a time for fellowship, for Bible study, for drawing closer to Him.

Not so long ago a number of the states in the U.S. had "Blue Laws" to prohibit profaning the Sabbath, but we have now reached a place where Sunday is business as usual – and few in leadership are crying out against that. Christian families, considering Sunday to be the Sabbath, are often divided on Sunday afternoons, with children going their ways and parents doing their things, sometimes the father playing golf and the mother doing something else. God named the Sabbath as the first Season of the Lord. How much longer will it be ignored?

Which day of the week we honor as the Sabbath is less important than honoring the Sabbath, but it should be noted that nothing in the New Testament changes the Sabbath from the apostles' practice of Friday at sundown to Saturday at sundown. Two Scriptures that supposedly say the first century Church celebrated the Sabbath on Sunday refer instead to Saturday evening, which was, and still is, called the First Day of the Week in Hebrew. In Acts 20:7. **And after sundown at the end of the Sabbath,** *with a service called Havdalah,* **when we gathered to break bread, Paul was speaking with them because he was planning to go on a journey the next day, and he was prolonging the message until midnight.** Paul was ministering at a service called Havdalah, and this is also what he referred to in 1 Corinthians 16:1. **And concerning the collection for the saints, as I ordered the congregations of Galatia, so also must you now do. 2. On Saturday evening at the Havdalah service each of you must now set aside for himself from** *your* **treasuries, whatever would be prospered, so that when I would come then collections would not need to be made.** Havdalah is the name of the service at the beginning of the day *after* the Sabbath. Havdalah is a Hebrew word meaning separation. Two hours after sundown ends the Sabbath, there is a service at the synagogue to make the transition back to the secular workday, and, after the Havdalah service, money can be handled. It was customary to share a meal immediately following this service. The two-hour delay for starting the service is to be absolutely certain that the Sabbath is over, with no chance for ending the Sabbath early. The Havdalah service is still held in synagogues around the world.

Isaiah 58:13. **If you restrain your foot because of the Sabbath, from pursuing your business on my holy day; and call the Sabbath a delight, the holy day of the Lord honorable; and shall honor it, not doing your own ways, nor pursuing your own business, nor speaking of vain matters; 14. (K) Then shall you delight yourself in the Lord; and I will cause you to ride upon the high places of the earth, and feed you with the heritage of Jacob your father; for the mouth of the Lord has spoken it.**

PASSOVER

Hebrew name: Pesach

Purpose: To remember God's deliverance from Egyptian
        bondage

Sabbath: No

Date: Nisan 14, which falls between mid-March and mid-
        April. In Scripture this month is called Aviv,
        meaning Spring.

Symbolized by a Seder plate, which has spaces for
each traditional item.

Leviticus 23:4. **These are the appointed seasons of
the Lord, even holy convocations, which ye shall
proclaim in their appointed season. 5. In the first
month, on the fourteenth day of the month at dusk,
is the Lord's Passover.**

Passover is the time when the blood of a lamb protected each home from the death of the firstborn. It's anniversary is the day when the Lamb of God, His Firstborn, gave Himself to protect us from spiritual bondage, to give us total freedom, salvation.

The lamb is killed immediately after sundown begins the fourteenth of Nisan. **Your lamb shall be without blemish, a male of the first year; you shall take it out from the sheep, or from the goats; And you shall keep it up until the fourteenth day of the same month; and the whole assembly of the congregation of Israel shall kill it in the evening.** (Exodus 12:5 & 6)

A meal called Seder is eaten on the fourteenth right after sundown according to the commands: **In the first month, on the fourteenth day of the month at evening, you shall eat unleavened bread, until the twenty first day of the month at dusk.** (Exodus 12:18)

Thus the meal is to be eaten on the fourteenth of Nisan. The Seder celebrates Passover with readings of the story of the trek through the wilderness, remembering all the bondage from which the Lord brought His children. Psalms and other songs are sung, making this a very festive evening with the Lord. During the Seder, the Passover meal, the story of the Exodus is told, based on Exodus 13:8. **And you shall tell your son in that day, saying, This is done because of that which the Lord did to me when I came forth out of Egypt.** 9. **And it shall be for a sign to you upon your hand, and for a memorial between your eyes, that the Lord's Torah may be in your mouth; for with a strong hand has the Lord brought you out of Egypt.** 10. **You shall therefore keep this ordinance in his season from year to year.** Verse 14 reinforces this, **And it shall be when your son asks you in time to come, saying, What is this? that you shall say to him, By strength of hand the Lord brought us out from Egypt, from the house of slavery;** This reminds all of us of the deliverance from Egyptian bondage and of the call of God upon our lives, with the giving of the Torah. The destination of the Exodus was the Promised Land. The purpose of the Exodus, the goal, was the creation of the Kingdom of Priests. Exodus 19:6. **And you shall be to me a kingdom of priests, and a holy nation...** Verse 10 says And **the Lord said to Moses, Go to the people, and sanctify them today and tomorrow, and let them wash their clothes.** Isaiah 61:6. **But you shall be named the Priests of the Lord; men shall call you the Ministers of our God; you shall eat the wealth of the nations, and in their riches you shall glory.** Israel is the Holy People, Leviticus 20:24, **But I have said to you, You shall inherit their land, and I will give it to you to possess it, a land that flows with milk and honey; I am the Lord your God, which have separated you from other people.** Leviticus 26:12, **And I will walk among you, and will be your God, and you shall be my people.** Deuteronomy 7:6. **For you are a holy people to the Lord your God; the Lord your God has chosen you to be a special people to himself, above all peoples that are upon the face of the earth.** Deuteronomy 14:2. **For you are a holy people to the Lord your God, and the Lord has chosen you to be a**

special people to himself, above all the nations that are upon the earth. Deuteronomy 28:9. **The Lord shall establish you as a holy people to himself, as he has sworn to you, if you shall keep the commandments of the Lord your God, and walk in his ways.** Paul tells us that we have been grafted in to this Holy People in Romans 11:17. **But if some of the branches were broken off, and you, since you are a wild olive, were yourself grafted in them, then you would be a participant for yourself of the richness of the root of the olive tree.** 18. **You must stop boasting of the branches: but, if you do boast, you do not support the root, but the root supports you.**

The Sabbath that falls immediately before Passover heightens the preparation for Passover. This day is called **The Great Sabbath, Shabbat HaGadol** in Hebrew, most likely because on this day the prophet Malachi is read in the synagogue, **Lo, I will send the prophet Elijah to you before the arrival of the Messiah.** The Messiah is expected during the coming feast. The rabbis have determined that Messiah's arrival will bring about the resurrection of the dead, expecting resurrection during this feast.

Passover is the primary feast of the Jewish year. While Scripture specifies one night, the 14th of the month Aviv, which is now called Nisan, outside of Israel Passover is celebrated for two nights. The meal is called Seder, a Hebrew word meaning Order, the first Seder on Nisan 14 in the synagogue, the second Seder on Nisan 15 in the home. This meal is not a feast in the sense of over-eating, but a modest, though ample, meal, often with roast chicken as the entree. Before the meal is served the story of the exodus from Egypt is told. The story is written in a booklet called Haggadah, a Hebrew word meaning Telling. Everyone in the home has been involved in the preparation that is necessary there, which includes spring cleaning to be sure all leaven is removed from the home. At the synagogue many are involved in the preparation, and everyone attending each Seder is involved in the telling.

Tradition has established certain symbols that supplement the Passover telling. These are:

18

Reclining, each celebrant is described as reclining, though few actually recline these days. Reclining represents freedom, luxury, and release from Egyptian slavery. The furnished room mentioned in Mark 14:15 would have had a low table with cushions around the table for the diners to recline while eating.

Lamb shank bone, roasted, represents the paschal sacrifice.

Bitter herbs, called Maror, represent the bitterness of their lives as slaves. Horseradish is normally used for this.

Haroset, a blend of fruit, nuts, and wine, represents the mortar they used when as slaves they put up buildings for Pharaoh.

Karpas, a vegetable, usually parsley or celery, to be dipped in salt water, represents the tears shed by the slaves.

Salt water or vinegar for the Karpas.

Red wine represents the blood of the lamb. Each celebrant dips a finger in his wine cup, and then places a drop of wine on his plate. Drops of wine are taken from the second cup of wine and placed on the plate to show sympathy with the Egyptians over their misery by diminishing the wine glass, because Scripture says **Wine makes the heart of man happy.** (Psalm 104:15) During the reading leading to the recitation of the plagues three drops are spilled at the mention of "blood and fire and pillars of smoke." Then one drop is taken or spilled for each of the ten plagues. This is repeated at the closing of the recitation when the leader says "D'tsach, Adash, B'Ahab". The first letters of the words for the plagues, summarizing the plagues, make these words. Thus a total of sixteen drops are spilled to show empathy with heathen suffering.

Matsah, the bread made without leaven, represents the haste in leaving Egypt and also the absence of sin, since leaven represents sin.

Matsah, made without leaven, resembles large

crackers. Three are taken to be used as

symbols. The middle one of these is broken in

half, with half, called *afikoman*, being wrapped in

a napkin and hidden until the end of the meal.

The afikoman is to be found by the children at

dessert time, who bargain with the adults for its

return. Afikoman is a Greek word meaning "I

have come."

Four questions are asked by children because

Exodus 13:14 says **And it shall be when your son**

asks you in time to come, saying, What is this? The

answers must be given so that the child can understand.

The questions are:

Why is this night different from all other nights?

1. Why, on all other nights, do we eat leavened

bread and Matsah; on this night we eat only

Matsah?

2. Why, on all other nights, do we eat all kinds of herbs: on this night, we eat mainly bitters?

3. Why, on all other nights, do we not dip even once; on this night, we dip twice?

4. Why on all other nights, do we eat either sitting straight or reclining; on this night, we all recline?

Four cups of wine are served. The rabbis of ancient times used wine to express covenant, so they used wine at the Seder as a reminder of these promises from Exodus 6:6. **Therefore say to the children of Yisrael, I am the Lord, and <u>I will bring you out</u> from under the burdens of Mitzraim (Egypt), and <u>I will deliver you</u> out of their bondage, and <u>I will redeem you</u> with an outstretched arm, and with great judgments: 7. and <u>I will take you to me</u> for a people, and I will be to you a God: and you shall know that I am the Lord your God, who brings you out from under the burdens of Mitzraim** (Egypt). (Jerusalem Bible, by Koren Publishing of Jerusalem)

Each cup represents a promise that was fulfilled in the Exodus:

1. and I will bring (v'hotseti) you out from under the burdens of Egypt.
2. and I will deliver (v'hitsalti) you out of their bondage
3. and I will redeem (v'galti) you with an outstretched arm
4. and I will take (v'lakachti) you to me for a people

Each "you" in these verses is plural, meaning these promises are for the whole body.

What we call **communion** is a very shortened form of the Seder, the Passover feast. Our Jewish brothers also have a shortened form of the Seder, but it is much longer than a communion. It is a service in the home every Friday evening called "Welcoming the Sabbath," which includes the four cups.

The rabbis teach that all the promises to Abraham apply to the wilderness, to Israel, and to the age to come. These promises to take us out from under the burdens of Egypt also apply to the wilderness, to Israel, and to the age to come.

Note that the first cup is the promise to take us out of Egypt, which today represents the world system. In the Seder, and in the home to welcome the Sabbath, this cup is called the Kiddush, the Sanctification, to sanctify the table in the home for the evening's service. In the Church today this is salvation as those who are born again leave the world system for the things of God.

The second cup is the deliverance from bondage, when the slavery ended, called the cup of Deliverance. Every member of the body is to be delivered from rejection, lust, low self-esteem, anger, jealously, depression, unforgiveness, and all the other ploys of the enemy. The vast majority of the Church has not understood this and does not accept deliverance, but deliverance is real and is for all who want it – and take it.

The third cup, the cup of Redemption, took place when the Red Sea opened for the Israelites, then closed to claim the Egyptian army. This is the first miracle to defy the laws of nature. It commemorates the physical departure from Egypt and speaks of the miracle of our redemption. Why does redemption follow deliverance? Many look at redemption as simply another word for salvation, but it is much more than that. Look at the book of Ruth to see the depth that the Lord has put in redemption. Just as Ruth was redeemed to intimacy with Boaz, we are redeemed for intimacy with God. His cry is for us to know Him, which means intimacy. God put deliverance first so we will be free to have true intimacy with Him.

The fourth cup, "I shall take you" reminds us of His carrying Israel through the desert and into the Promised Land. It also speaks of our walk with Him and His taking us into eternal life.

A special cup is used for Elijah. This fourth cup is called the Cup of Elijah, and is poured for Elijah to drink. The youngest child who is able goes to the door to see if Elijah is coming to herald the Messiah.

We are to grasp each time we take communion that we are drinking the cup as spoken by Jesus in Luke 22:20. **Then likewise the cup after they ate, saying, "This is the cup of the New Covenant in My blood which is being poured out on your behalf."**

The Seder and home service welcoming Shabbat close with the singing of Psalms 113 through 118, along with other appropriate songs. Psalms 113-118 are called "The Hallel," meaning Praise.

A Seder Haggadah is much more detailed than this brief outline. If you would like one, you can usually find one on either the coffee aisle or Jewish section in any supermarket the weeks before Passover. Maxwell House Coffee distributes these every year.

Reclining is not understood by most of us since we

always sit at a table. This passage from John 13 is an example: 23. **One of His disciples, whom Jesus loved, was next to Jesus.** 24. **Then Simon Peter beckoned to him to ask whoever might be the one about whom He was speaking.** 25. **So that one, in front of Jesus, said to Him, "Lord, who is it?"** These are often translated "leaning on Jesus' bosom" (verse 23) and "lying on Jesus' breast" (verse 25), but these are idioms referring to the person next to or in front of someone. The couches or cushions were placed at an angle to the table so each person would not take up more than one space at the table. Each would lie on one side, which meant that the next person would be in front, spoken of as being or lying on the bosom of that person.

Luke 16 has another reference to this: 23. **And in Hades, as he was in torment, when he lifted up his eyes he saw Abraham from afar and Lazarus in his bosom.** There are two meanings for being in the bosom of Abraham. For people on earth it means to be in the place of honor at a banquet. For those in heaven it means to share the bliss that Abraham enjoys, as the saint reclines in front of Abraham at the heavenly banquet table.

Now, however, I am on my way to Jerusalem in the service of the saints there. For Macedonia and Achaia were pleased to make a contribution for the poor among the saints in Jerusalem. They were pleased to do it, and indeed they owe it to them. For if the Gentiles have shared in the Jews' spiritual blessings, they owe it to the Jews to share with them their material blessings. (Romans 15:25-27) It is an indisputable fact that everything pertaining to salvation has come to us through the Jewish people: the patriarchs, the prophets, the Bible, our Savior, the apostles, the gospel and the church.

Nothing connects the church more clearly to Israel and her Jewish roots than the Feast of Passover. This first of the feasts of the Lord is celebrated in memory of the great exodus out of Egypt through the blood of the Lamb. But it was also during the last Passover meal

together with His Jewish disciples, in celebration of this
exodus out from Egypt, that Jesus instituted the new
covenant in His own blood, a celebration we now call
communion.

**When the hour came, Jesus and his apostles
reclined at the table. And He said to them, 'I have
greatly desired *with* a longing to eat this Seder with
you before I suffer: 16. for I say to you that I would
<u>not</u> eat it *again* until this would be fulfilled in the
kingdom of God.' 17. Then having taken a cup, after
He gave thanks, He said, 'You must take this and
you must immediately share *it* among yourselves:
18. for I say to you, that from now on I am <u>not</u>
drinking from this product of the vine until the
kingdom of God would come.' 19. Then having
taken bread, after He gave thanks, He broke *it* and
gave *it* to them saying, 'This is My body which is
being given on your behalf: you must continually do
this in My remembrance.' 20. Then likewise the cup**

after they ate, saying, 'This *is* the cup of the New Covenant (Jer 31:31-34) in My blood which is being poured out on your behalf.' Luke 22:14-20

How has the Church paid back its debt to the Jewish people? Already in 196 AD, a council meeting in Caesarea, where no Jewish believers were present, determined that the resurrection of Jesus should be celebrated on a Sunday during the Feast of Eshtar, a pagan goddess, instead of during the third day of Passover on the Feast of First Fruits, (see Leviticus 23:9-11 and 1 Corinthians 15:4,20-23).

At the universal Council of Nicea I in 325 AD this practice became official dogma. The decision was based on the argumentation that it is not fitting for the Church in her celebration of the Lord's death and resurrection to be connected with the cursed Jewish nation that crucified Him. And so it has remained ever since. How sad and tragic that the Church that God has called to provoke Israel to jealousy abandoned her Jewish roots and identity. We have in this way robbed our Savior and Messiah of His Jewishness, of His having lived His whole life as an observant Jew!

It is time today for the Church to pay back her huge spiritual debt to the Jewish people, a debt that has multiplied over 1800 years of racial hatred, bigotry and bloody atrocities committed against them by the Church.

Just as Israel gave birth to the Church in the first century, the Church is called to give birth to Israel in the last. We strongly believe that it would honor the Lord, if during Passover, churches gather together around a Passover Seder meal and communion to remember our Jewish roots and our debt towards the Jewish people for our salvation, continuing with an all night prayer meeting.

Jesus spent that night with His disciples in prayer. We, too, should spend that night in prayer for salvation of the world, so that the entire world would worship the King of the Universe. **Because the LORD kept vigil that night to bring them out of Egypt, on this night all the Israelites are to keep vigil to honor the LORD**

for the generations to come. Exodus 12:42 **Brothers, my heart's desire and prayer to God for the Israelites is that they may be saved.** Romans 10:1 **For if their rejection is the reconciliation of the world, what will their acceptance be but life from the dead?** Romans 11:15

The Seder meal so graphically illustrates our salvation through Jesus' death and resurrection. We should remember that during the same night basically every Jewish person in the world, whether religious or not, is also gathered around a Seder meal, just like they have done every year, for almost 3,500 years. It is in fact the oldest continuously observed religious feast in existence today.

We know that identification is one of the strongest keys to effective intercession. Coming together, preferably in unity as a citywide church, around a Seder Meal with Communion during Passover is then a very powerful tool in intercession for revival in Israel.

UNLEAVENED BREAD

Hebrew name: Hag Hamatsot

Purpose: Tell the children of God's mighty hand bringing
deliverance to Israel

Sabbath: Partial, no labor, first and seventh days

Date: Nisan 15, March or April, begins the day after
Passover, lasts seven days.   In the Torah this
month is called Aviv, the Hebrew word for Spring.

Symbolized by matzah bread, which is eaten not only on
Passover, but also throughout the entire Feast of
Unleavened Bread.

Today Passover and Unleavened Bread combined
are often just called Passover. The emphasis is on

freedom from bondage, for the purpose of worshipping God.

Leviticus 23:6. **And on the fifteenth day of the same month is the Feast of Unleavened Bread to the Lord; seven days you must eat unleavened bread.** 7. **In the first day you shall have a holy gathering; you shall do no labor in it.** 8. **But you shall offer an offering made by fire to the Lord seven days; in the seventh day is a holy gathering; you shall do no labor in it.** This command to do no labor is different from the command in Exodus 20:8-10, in which we are told not to do any manner of work on the Sabbath. During a feast day Sabbath it is forbidden to work at your job because the Scripture says to "do no labor" but unlike the seventh day of the week, it is permissible to do a chore around the house, within reason. Even this partial Sabbath is to be spent with the Lord, so taking the day to paint your house or plant your garden would be way out of line. To do something that would break the peace would be improper, like mowing the lawn or using a chain saw.

The feast begins at sundown Nisan 15 with the second Seder, this one celebrated in the home. This second Seder is not a Scriptural mandate, but traditional.

The Rabbis teach that resurrection for judgment takes place during the Feast of Unleavened Bread. Jesus was resurrected during Unleavened Bread, on First Fruits. Please note that Judgment Day takes place several months later, on Rosh Hashanah, the Day of Memorial. (See Chart at the back of the book.)

The seventh, the last day of Unleavened Bread calls to mind the parting of the Red Sea. The chronology of the first week of the exodus is:

Nisan 15, traveled from Ramses to Sukkot

Nisan 16, traveled from Sukkot to Eitam (Exodus 13:20)

Nisan 17, retreated toward Egypt, camped at Pihakhirot
        (Exodus 14:2)

Nisan 18, Pharaoh's agents reported that three days had
        gone by and they were not returning
        (Exodus 14:5)

Nisan 19, 20, Pharaoh organized forces &
pursued the Jewish people (Exodus 14:6-10)
Nisan 21, Red Sea split, allowing Israelites to escape.
(Exodus 14:13-16)

FIRST FRUITS

Hebrew name: Resheet K'tsirchem, Beginning of Your
Harvest, or Your First Harvest.

Purpose: Offering of First Fruits

Sabbath: No

Date: Nisan 16, March or April, second day of
Unleavened Bread. The month now called Nisan
was called Aviv in Scripture.

Symbolized by a basket of fruit because this offering
was brought in a basket. Although this basket has fruit,
barley is the crop harvested just before this First Fruits,
so the basket would normally have held barley. There
are three First Fruits celebrations each year.

Leviticus 23:9. **And the Lord spoke to Moses,
saying,** 10. **Speak to the people of Israel, and say to
them, When you come to the land which I give to**

you, and shall reap its harvest, then you shall bring a sheaf of the first fruits of your harvest to the priest; 11. And he shall wave the sheaf before the Lord, to be accepted for you; on the next day after the Sabbath the priest shall wave it. 12. And you shall offer that day when you wave the sheaf a male lamb without blemish of the first year for a burnt offering to the Lord. 13. And the meal offering of it shall be two tenth deals of fine flour mixed with oil, an offering made by fire to the Lord for a sweet savor; and the drink offering of it shall be of wine, the fourth part of a hin. 14. And you shall eat nor bread, nor parched grain, nor green ears, until the same day that you have brought an offering to your God; it shall be a statute forever throughout your generations in all your dwellings.

Each First Fruits of the three harvest festivals is joyful, filled with thanksgiving. The quantities brought to the temple were not specified, and were never a great quantity; one basket carried a family's offering, although a king brought a basket that required two to carry it. Deuteronomy 26:2. tells us the offering should be brought in a basket. Deuteronomy 26:1. **And it shall be, when you come in to the land which the Lord your God gives you for an inheritance, and possess it, and live in it; 2. That you shall take of the first of all the fruit of the earth, which you shall bring of your land that the Lord your God gives you, and shall put it in a basket, and shall go to the place which the Lord your God shall choose to place his name there. 3. And you shall go to the priest who shall be in those days, and say to him, I declare this day to the Lord your God, that I have come to the country which the Lord swore to our fathers to give us. 4. And the priest shall take the basket from your hand, and set it down before the altar of the Lord your God.**

The offering was presented as described in Deuteronomy 26:2, then the one presenting would make this statement from Deuteronomy 26:5. And you shall speak and say before the Lord your God, 'A wandering Aramean was my father, and he went down into Egypt, and sojourned there with a few, and became there a nation, great, mighty, and populous; 6. And the Egyptians dealt ill with us, and afflicted us, and laid upon us hard slavery; 7. And when we cried to the Lord God of our fathers, the Lord heard our voice, and looked on our affliction, and our labor, and our oppression; 8. And the Lord brought us out of Egypt with a mighty hand, and with an outstretched arm, and with great awesomeness, and with signs, and with wonders; 9. And he has brought us to this place, and has given us this land, a land that flows with milk and honey. 10. And now, behold, I have brought the first fruits of the land, which you, O Lord, have given me.' And you shall set it before the Lord your God, and worship before the Lord your God; 11. And you shall rejoice in every good thing which the Lord your God has given to you, and to your house, you, and the Levite, and the stranger who is among you. The portion in quotes, verses 5-10, was repeated by each one bringing a First Fruits offering to the temple.

The produce offered at First Fruits are defined in Deuteronomy 8:8. **A land of wheat, barley, vines (grapes), fig trees, and pomegranates; a land of olive oil, and date-honey.** These were the only crops offered for First Fruits. During the Feast of Unleavened Bread barley was the crop that was being harvested, so that is what would have been brought, although someone who had not been able to come to the previous First Fruits could bring that offering at the next First Fruits. This modest offering from just a few crops expresses commitment to God and thanksgiving to Him for His provision.

The Feast of Unleavened Bread closes with the reading of Psalm 93: 3. **The floods have lifted up, O Lord, the floods have lifted up their voice; the floods lift up their roaring.** 4. **The Lord on high is mightier than the noise of many waters, than the mighty waves of the sea.** This is because Exodus 14:13-16 shows that it was on the seventh day that the Israelites crossed the Red Sea on their way out of Egypt.

The Counting of the Omer, counting fifty days from the First Fruits of Unleavened Bread to the First Fruits of Shavuot, ties first Fruits of Unleavend Bread to the next Season. Omer means sheaf and these first two of the First Fruits were offerings for the harvesting of barley, then of wheat at the Feast of Shavuot at the end of counting the fifty days.

Jesus was resurrected on the First Fruits of Unleavened Bread, then forty days later He ascended, and ten days after that, on Shavuot, the Holy Spirit was given. Thus the fifty days of Counting the Omer tie His resurrection, ascension, and the giving of the baptism of the Holy Spirit.

WEEKS

Hebrew name: Shavuot, pronounced Sha-**voo**-ote.

Purpose: Offering of First Fruits

Sabbath: Partial, no labor.

Date: Sivan, mid-May to mid-June, seven weeks plus
      one day after the First Fruits of Unleavened Bread.

Symbolized by the basket, which at Shavuot would have held the wheat recently harvested.

Leviticus 23:15. **And you shall count from the next day after the Sabbath, from the day that you brought the sheaf of the wave offering; seven Sabbaths shall be complete;** 16. **To the next day after the seventh Sabbath shall you count fifty days; and you shall offer a new meal offering to the Lord.** 17. **You shall** bring out of your habitations two wave loaves of two tenth deals; they shall be of fine flour; they shall be baked with leaven; they are the first fruits to the Lord. 18. And you shall offer with the bread seven lambs without blemish of the first year, and one young bull, and two rams; they shall be for a burnt offering to the Lord, with their meal offering, and their drink offerings, an offering made by fire, of sweet savor to the Lord. 19. Then you shall sacrifice one kid of the goats for a sin offering, and two lambs of the first year for a sacrifice of peace offerings. 20. And the priest shall wave them with the bread of the first fruits for a wave offering before the Lord with the two lambs; they shall be holy to the Lord for the priest. 21. And you shall proclaim on the same day, that it may be a holy gathering to you; you shall do no labor in it; it shall be a statute forever in all your dwellings throughout your generations. 22. And when you reap the harvest of your land, you shall not make clean riddance up to the corners of your field when you reap, nor shall

you gather any gleaning of your harvest; you shall leave them to the poor, and to the stranger; I am the Lord your God.

This commandment to leave the corners and not to glean is the only commandment in Leviticus 23 that deals with something other than these special days. The reason for this command is that this reminds the farmer that the crop is not his, but the Lord's.

The Feast of Weeks is not on a specific date, but the start of it is determined by counting the weeks, seven weeks plus one day, which is why it is called Weeks. The Greek name is Pentecost, meaning fifty, for the fifty days or seven weeks plus one day. Counting the days between them ties the two First Fruits together, just as Jesus ties His resurrection, ascension, and the giving of the baptism of the Holy Spirit at the Feast of Weeks, called Pentecost, its Greek name, by many Christians.

Exodus 19:1 tells us that in the third month, the month of Shavuot, the people were at Sinai. The rest of the chapter tells how He gave the Torah to His people there. For this reason Weeks, Shavuot, also celebrates the giving of Torah. The emphasis on Torah brings to mind the statement **..You shall have no other gods before Me.** This means we must leave <u>all</u> our idols behind, which is hard to do in this materialistic, Nicolaiton, Humanist, pleasure-filled age. Old habits die hard, seen with the children of Israel in the wilderness, and in our focus on material things instead of doing the things Jesus brings out in Matthew 25:35. **For I was hungry and you gave Me to eat, I was thirsty and you gave Me to drink, I was a stranger and you took Me in,** 36. **and *I was* poorly clothed and you clothed Me, I was sick and you visited Me, I was in prison and you came to Me.**

Because in Exodus 19:8 all the people answering said, **All that the Lord has spoken we will do..** and this was on Shavuot; this day is likened to a wedding, tying His people permanently to Him.

DAYS OF AWE

Also called The High Holy Days

Hebrew name: Aseret Yemei Teshuvah (Ten Days of
Repentance)

Purpose: Ten days of repentance to prepare for Yom
Kippur

Date: First ten days of Tishrei, late August to late
September.

Symbolized by the Torah scroll, featured in the call to
repentance and a vow to be better in the coming year.

Days of Awe is the name of the days from Rosh
HaShanah to Yom Kippur, the days when each person is
to focus on repentance and on being a better person the
coming year than the year just ended. Each of us

needs to be like David, *I considered my ways.* (Psalm 119:59) David knew he was not perfect: each of us must recognize that since the beginning of time only One Perfect Being has walked the earth – and that was our Messiah.

DAY OF MEMORIAL

Hebrew name: Zichron (Memorial or Remembrance),
Rosh HaShanah (New Year)

Purpose: To remember all that God has done for you, to respond to the call to repentance.

Sabbath: Partial, no labor.

Date: Tishrie 1, from late August to late September.

Symbolized by a shofar, which issues the call to repentance, plus a prayer shawl and tefilin, which represent each individual's commitment and relationship with the Lord.

While this is sometimes referred to as the Feast of Trumpets, Scripture does not call this a feast, and a trumpet is not mentioned in the Hebrew text. The shofar is blown as a call to repentance. Leviticus 23:23. **And the Lord spoke to Moses, saying,** 24. **Speak to the people of Israel, saying, In the seventh month, in the first day of the month, shall you have a Sabbath, a memorial of blowing of horns, a holy gathering.** 25. **You shall do no labor in it; but you shall offer an offering made by fire to the Lord.**

This Day of Memorial is for us to remember all the things that God has done for us, a time of reflection in preparation for the Day of Atonement. The ten days after the Day of Memorial are to be dedicated to repentance, getting ready for the Day of Atonement.

Tradition has this day as the anniversary of Creation, which is how this day came to be known as Rosh Hashanah, New Year. Years are reckoned from this day, while months are counted from Nisan, Passover.

Tradition also has the Day of Memorial as Judgment Day. Matthew 16: 27. **For the Son of Man is going to come in the glory of His Father with His angels, and**

then He will give back to each according to his actions.

The focus of the synagogue service is prayer and repentance. There are services the first evening, the next morning, then a late afternoon service which has a custom called "Tashlikh," meaning "cast," during which sins are cast into the sea. This is based on Micah 7:19. **He will again have compassion upon us; he will suppress our iniquities; and you will cast all their sins into the depths of the sea.** The whole congregation throws bread into the nearest sea, lake, or river. **Cast your bread upon the waters..** (Ecclesiastes 11:1) and Micah 7:19 says **..You will cast all their sins into the depths of the sea.** The water needs to be flowing water to represent the washing away of sin. The waters of Rosh Hashanah symbolize the creation of the world and its new beginning, as with each individual and the casting away of sin. Implicit in this is a call for forgiveness, for each to forgive everyone of everything each has against someone. Another service follows this brief service, and yet another the following morning.

True repentance cannot bear fruit until the repentant person forgives every one of every little thing and every big thing. Nothing can be held back. Matthew 6:12. **You must right now forgive our sins for us, in the same manner as we have completed forgiving everyone of everything, big and little, against us:**
(Verse 13 omitted)
14. **For if you would forgive *all other* people their transgressions, your heavenly Father will also forgive you: 15. but if you would not forgive *all other* people, neither will your Father forgive your sins.**

The Rosh Hashanah service in many synagogues begins with a call for each one there to forgive everyone of everything, no matter how big or small. Forgiveness by every believer must take place before the process of atonement can begin, being completed on the Day of Atonement.

The Day of Memorial celebration lasts two days because it is so difficult to precisely determine the day for the new moon, the First of Tishrei. Any other month is less critical than Tishrei for this determination.

At meals and snacks round loaves of hallah bread symbolize the ongoing cycle of life. Dipping pieces of bread or apples in honey speaks of hope for a sweet year.

Shabbat Shuva

(No Scriptural Reference)

The Sabbath between Rosh Hashanah and Yom Kippur is called Shabbat Shuva, Sabbath of Return. Return refers to repentance, the Hebrew word for repentance being T'shuva. Since this is not in Leviticus 23 this is not listed like the rest of the Days in this book.

DAY OF ATONEMENT

Hebrew name: Yom Kippur

Purpose: Repentance, forgiveness of sins

Sabbath: Called Shabbat Shabbattone (Sabbath of
Sabbaths, Holiest Day of the Year), Full
Sabbath, and no manner of work.

Date: Tishrei 10, early September to early October.

Symbolized by a mezuzah case and scroll, representing
the entire household's restatement of commitment. The
mezuzah, a case containing Scriptures, is attached to
the doorframe. The Scriptures are Deuteronomy 6:4-9,
11:13-21, and Numbers 15:37-41. These are called the
Sh'ma Yisrael, which means, "Hear, O Israel.."

Leviticus 23:26. **And the Lord spoke to Moses,
saying,** 27. **Also on the tenth day of this seventh
month there shall be a day of atonement; it shall be**

a holy gathering to you; and you shall afflict your souls, and offer an offering made by fire to the Lord. 28. And you shall do no work in that same day; for it is a day of atonement, to make atonement for you before the Lord your God. 29. For whatever soul it is who shall not be afflicted in that same day, he shall be cut off from among his people. 30. And whatever soul it is who does any work in that same day, the same soul will I destroy from among his people. 31. You shall do no kind of work; it shall be a statute forever throughout your generations in all your dwellings. 32. It shall be to you a Sabbath of rest, and you shall afflict your souls; in the ninth day of the month at evening, from evening to evening, shall you celebrate your Sabbath.

This day is a full Sabbath, and a full fast, with not even water from sundown to sundown. Regarding work, this is the only Season of the Lord with the same restrictions as the weekly Sabbath. The purpose of this day is to repent for not being as good a person as you could have been the year just ended, and to vow to be better during the year just starting. The shofar is blown as a call to repentance, which Christians still need. Most Christians are free from sins of immorality, murder, theft, but none of us in perfect. We all sin with our speech, saying things that hurt others – often not aware that the other is offended. We also fail to lift up someone who needs an encouraging word. This is sin, without even mentioning jealousy, greed, pride, gossip, slander, or lust. Each one needs to be more sensitive to the Spirit so we can truly let God's love shine through us more and more, increasing year by year.

It is important for Christians to recognize that even though we are made righteous by faith and by the blood of the Lamb, we are not to be presumptuous, because none of us has been perfected and we all need to be better this coming year than we have been the year now ending. It is this desire to truly be the people God wants us to be that drives us to walk in repentance every day of the year, but to be especially watchful during this time that His instructions have established a season of repentance, to remember all that God has done for each of us and to strive to be better the coming year.

Said Rabbi Jose: "For this reason it behooves man to be on his guard against sin and to turn neither to the right nor to the left; and however careful he may be, he should still search himself daily for any sin. When a man rises in the morning two witnesses join him and follow him the whole day. When he opens his eyes, they say to him: **Let thine eyes look right on, and let thine eyelids look straight before thee** (Proverbs 4:25); when he gets up and makes ready to walk, they say to him: **Make plain the paths of thy feet,..** (Proverbs 4:26). A man, therefore, should be on his guard against his sins the whole day and every day, and when night comes it behooves him to look back and examine all the actions he has done that day, so that he may repent. So David said: **And my sin is ever before me** (Psalm 51:5), as an exhortation to repentance."

The Yom Kippur service starts before sundown with a service called Kol Nidrei, meaning All Vows. The focus of this service, which has been part of Yom Kippur since the eighth century, is a religious court called Beit Din, which renounces legally all vows. The specific vows that created the need for this service were the courts of the Christian nations where the Jewish people lived, requiring the Jewish people to convert to Christianity. Often the alternatives for those asked to take the vows were to be killed or to have their children taken away to be raised by Christians. Because the Kol Nidrei is a "court" it is necessary to have the service before sundown because sundown starts the Sabbath, when the court must be adjourned.

BOOTHS

Hebrew name: Sukkot (Booths)

　Alternate English name: Tabernacles

Purpose: First Fruits, Fall Harvest

Sabbaths: Partial, first and seventh days

Date: Tishrei 15, mid-September to mid-October.

Leviticus 23:33. **And the Lord spoke to Moses, saying,** 34. **Speak to the people of Israel, saying, The fifteenth day of this seventh month shall be the Feast of Booths for seven days to the Lord.** 35. **On the first day shall be a holy gathering; you shall do no labor in it.** 36. **Seven days you shall offer an offering made by fire to the Lord; on the eighth day shall be a holy gathering to you; and you shall offer an offering made by fire to the Lord; it is a solemn assembly; and you shall do no labor in it.**

The Feast of Booths begins at sundown on Tishrei 15. Christians traditionally call this the Feast of Tabernacles, but the correct term is Feast of Booths because the Hebrew word used is Sukkot, referring to the flimsy shelters called for, and it has no relationship to either the tabernacle in the wilderness or to David's tabernacle.

Booths are made, based on Leviticus 23:42. **You shall dwell in booths seven days; all who are Israelites born shall dwell in booths;** 43. **That your generations may know that I made the people of Israel to dwell in booths, when I brought them out of the land of Egypt; I am the Lord your God.** 44. **And Moses declared to the people of Israel the feasts of the Lord.**

These booths are made from palm fronds or leafy branches, and are not to be very stable, not good protection. Men are to live in the booths the entire time of the feast. Women have the option of living in the house or staying in the booth, although meals are to be eaten in the booth. Meals are shared with friends, neighbors, and especially the poor. The entire feast is celebrated as a family, doing everything together. The children are involved in every aspect, including the spiritual guests.

Nehemiah 8:17,18 **And all the congregation of those who were come back out of the captivity made booths, and dwelt in the booths: for since the days of Yeshua (Joshua) the son of Nun to that day the children of Yisra'el (Israel) had not done so. And there was very great gladness. Also day-by-day, from the first day to the last day, he read in the book of the Torah of God. And they kept the feast seven days; and on the eighth day was a solemn assembly, according to the prescribed form.** (Jerusalem Bible, Koren Publishing, Jerusalem)

On the first day the reading from the Prophets is Zechariah 14:1-17 1. **Behold, the day of the Lord comes, and the plunder taken from you shall be divided in your midst. 2. (K) For I will gather all nations against Jerusalem to battle; and the city shall be taken, and the houses rifled, and the women** raped; and half of the city shall go into Exodus, and the remnant of the people shall not be cut off from the city. 3. Then shall the Lord go forth, and fight against those nations, as when he fought in the day of battle. 4. And his feet shall stand on that day upon the Mount of Olives, which is before Jerusalem on the east, and the Mount of Olives shall be split in its midst toward the east and toward the west, and there shall be a very great valley; and half of the mountain shall be moved toward the north, and half of it toward the south. 5. And you shall flee to the valley of the mountains; for the valley of the mountains shall reach to Azal; yes, you shall flee, like you fled from the earthquake in the days of Uzziah king of Judah; and the Lord my God shall come, and all the holy ones with you. 6. (K) And it shall come to pass on that day, that there shall not be bright light nor thick darkness; 7. But it shall be one day which shall be known to the Lord, not day, nor night; but it shall come to pass, that at evening time there shall be light. 8. And it shall be on that day, that living waters shall go out from Jerusalem; half of them toward the eastern sea, and half of them toward the western sea; in summer and in winter shall it be. 9. And the Lord shall be king over all the earth; on that day the Lord shall be one, and his name one. 10. All the land shall be changed like the Arabah from Geba to Rimmon south of Jerusalem; and she shall be lifted up, and remain in her place, from the Gate of Benjamin to the place of the first gate, to the Corner Gate, and from the Tower of Hananeel to the king's wine presses. 11. And men shall dwell in it, and there shall be no more utter destruction; but Jerusalem shall dwell secure. 12. And this shall be the plague with which the Lord will strike all the people who fought against Jerusalem; Their flesh shall consume away while they stand upon their feet, and their eyes shall consume away in their sockets, and their tongue shall consume away in their mouth. 13. And it shall come to pass on that day, that a great panic from the Lord shall be among them; and they shall lay hold everyone on the hand of his neighbor, and his hand shall rise up against the hand of his neighbor. 14. And Judah also shall fight at Jerusalem; and the wealth of all the nations around shall be gathered together, gold, and silver, and clothing, in great abundance. 15. And such shall be the plague of the horse, of the mule, of the camel, and of the ass, and of all the beasts that shall be in these camps, as this plague. 16. And it shall come to pass, that everyone who is left of all the nations which came against Jerusalem shall go up from year to year to worship the King, the Lord of hosts, and to keep the Feast of Booths. 17. And it shall be, that whoever will not come up of all the families of the earth to Jerusalem to worship the King, the Lord of hosts, upon them shall be no rain.

Jesus celebrated Sukkot. John 7: 2. **And the Feast of Booths of the Jewish people was near.** John 7:10. **And as His brothers went up to the feast, then He also went up, not openly, but in secret.**

Jesus honored every season of the Lord and never suggested any changes for them. No author of the New Testament suggested changing any of these seasons.

Sukkot, or Booths, is the third **First Fruits** of the seasons, the Fall harvest. The first fruits are to be brought in a basket, as described in First Fruits during Unleavened Bread, page 37.

The Feast begins! The Trumpets are blown for the first time since the first of the month Elul, the month before Rosh Hashanah. Rosh Hashanah and Yom Kippur are announced by the shofar, the call to repentance. The trumpet, however, is a call to rejoice, and a call to war.

The war is against Gog, which means roof in Hebrew, with man relying on a strong, solid roof, not the flimsy roof of a booth, or sukkah. The heavenly hosts defeat Gog and Magog – a solid roof could not make mankind safe and secure against that which comes from above.

The sages wrote that Psalm 2 speaks of the war of Gog and Magog:

> 1. **Why do the nations rage, and the peoples mutter a vain thing?** 2. **The kings of the earth set themselves, and the rulers take counsel together, against the Lord, and against his anointed, saying,** 3. **Let us break their bonds asunder, and cast away their cords from us.** 4. **He who sits in the heavens shall laugh: the Lord shall have them in derision.** 5. **Then he shall speak to them in his wrath, and terrify them in his fury.** 6. **But I have set my king on my holy mountain of Zion.** 7. **I will tell of the decree; the Lord has said to me, You are my son; this day have I begotten you.**

These are brought out in more detail in Ezekiel

38:18. **And it shall come to pass on that day, when Gog shall come against the land of Israel, says the Lord God, that my fury shall be roused.** 19. **For in my jealousy and in the fire of my wrath have I spoken, Surely in that day there shall be a great shaking in the land of Israel;** 20. **And the fishes of the sea, and the birds of the sky, and the beasts of the field, and all creeping things that creep upon the earth, and all the men who are upon the face of the earth, shall tremble at my presence, and the mountains shall be thrown down, and the steep places shall fall, and every wall shall fall to the ground.** 21. **And I will call for a sword against him throughout all my mountains, says the Lord God; every man's sword shall be against his brother.** 22. **And I will contend with him by pestilence and by blood; and I will rain down upon him, and upon his bands, and upon the many people that are with him, a torrential rain, and great hailstones, fire, and brimstone.** 23. **Thus will I magnify myself, and sanctify myself; and I will make myself known in the** eyes of many nations, and they shall know that I am the Lord.

Ezekiel 39. 1. **And you, son of man, prophesy against Gog, and say, Thus said the Lord God; Behold, I am against you, O Gog, the chief prince of Meshech and Tubal;** 2. **And I will turn you around, and entice you on, and will cause you to come up from the farthest north, and will bring you against the mountains of Israel;** 3. **And I will strike your bow from your left hand, and will cause your arrows to fall from your right hand.** 4. **You shall fall upon the mountains of Israel, you, and all your bands, and the peoples that are with you; I will give you to the ravenous birds of every sort, and to the beasts of the field to be devoured.** 5. **You shall fall upon the open field; for I have spoken it, says the Lord God.** 6. **And I will send a fire on Magog, and among those who dwell securely in the islands; and they shall know that I am the Lord.** 7. **And I will I make my holy name known in the midst of my people Israel; and I** will not let them profane my holy name any more; and the nations shall know that I am the Lord, the Holy One in Israel. 8. Behold, it has come, and it is done, says the Lord God; this is the day of which I have spoken. 9. And those who dwell in the cities of Israel shall go forth, and shall set on fire and burn the weapons, both the shields and the bucklers, the bows and the arrows, and the staves, and the spears, and they shall burn them with fire for seven years; 10. And they shall take no wood from the field, nor cut down any from the forests; for they shall burn the weapons with fire; and they shall destroy those who destroyed them, and rob those who robbed them, says the Lord God. 11. And it shall come to pass in that day, that I will give to Gog a place for burial in Israel, the Valley of the Travelers to the east of the sea; and it shall block the path of the travelers; and there shall they bury Gog and all his multitude; and they shall call it the Valley of Hamon-Gog, (Multitude of Gog). 12. For seven months shall the house of Israel bury them, so that

they may cleanse the land. 13. And all the people of the land shall bury them; and it shall be to them a renown on the day that I shall be glorified, says the Lord God. 14. And they shall set apart men of continual employment, passing through the land to bury with the travelers those who remain upon the face of the earth, so as to cleanse it; after the end of seven months shall they search. 15. And the travelers who pass through the land, when any sees human bone, then he shall set up a sign by it, till the grave diggers have buried it in the valley of Hamon-Gog. 16. And also the name of the city shall be Hamonah. Thus shall they cleanse the land.

There is an inner connection between the names Gog and Magog and the feast, Sukkot. The Hebrew word, Gog, means roof, and there is a major difference between a real roof and the flimsy sukkah, the singular of Sukkot. The sukkah is a weak, unstable shelter made with branches. A driving rain will soak right through it. A driving wind will blow it away. People have the power to make themselves safe and secure against their earthly contemporaries by building sturdy walls, so they delude themselves into thinking that they can make themselves safe and secure against that which comes from above – against God and His power to direct matters. They think that they can find security in the protection of their own might, take their fate in their own hands, and crown the building of human greatness with gabled roofs,

rendering them independent of God.

The war of Gog and Magog is the battle of gog, *roof*, against sukkah, the fight of the roof-illusion, of human greatness which never allows rest, against the sukkah-truth of cheerful confidence and serenity which comes from placing one's trust in God's protection. Magog is gog with the prefix M. This prefix expresses the idea of projecting something, representing the philosophy that man can insulate himself against the heavenly power of God – Magog is the attempt to project this philosophy on Earth. *This explanation of Gog-Magog is adapted from the Stone Edition Chumash, and is true today as the Lord's greatest enemy on Earth is Humanism.*

In celebrating Sukkot each celebrant carries a collection of branches, called Lulav. The Lulav is taken to the Western Wall in Jerusalem according to the following Scripture: Leviticus 23:40. **And you shall take on the first day the boughs of goodly trees, branches of palm trees, and the boughs of thick trees, and willows of the brook; and you shall rejoice before the Lord your God seven days.**

Tradition uses Four Species as very important symbols. The two best known symbols speak of unity, unity of purpose and unity of the Jewish people, as follows.

First, the citron equals the heart; the palm branch, the spine; the three myrtle leaves, the eye; the two willows, the mouth. Note that the total number of items in this is seven. The palm branch and the three myrtle leaves are held in one hand, the citron and two willows in the other. These are waved to the North, South, East, and West to show that every corner of the earth belongs to God. This is a parallel to the seventy bulls offered being meant to secure blessings for the seventy nations of the ancient world.

Second, the **etrog**, having both taste and a pleasant aroma, symbolizes one who both knows Scripture and does good deeds. The **lulav**, a branch of the date palm whose fruit has a taste but no aroma, symbolizes someone who knows Scripture but does not do good deeds. The **myrtle**, having no taste but does have an aroma, symbolizes a person who does not know Scripture but does good deeds. The **willow**, having neither taste nor aroma, symbolizes the person who neither knows Scripture nor does good deeds. Just as in the Church, all four kinds are included in Israel.

Those worshippers not in Jerusalem carry these Lulav to the synagogue and wave them while reciting Psalms 113-118. They walk in procession around the inside of the synagogue seven times, chanting prayers for deliverance. The basis for this is Joshua marching around Jericho seven times on the seventh day.

And the Lord will create upon every dwelling place of mount Zion, and upon her assemblies, a cloud and smoke by day, and the shining of a

flaming fire by night; for upon all the glory shall be a canopy. 6. **And there shall be a booth for a shadow in the daytime from the heat, and for a place of refuge, and for a covert from storm and from rain.** Isaiah 4:5,6.

The first day, from sundown to sundown the next day, is a Sabbath, but feast day Sabbaths are partial Sabbaths. The partial Sabbath is noted in Leviticus 23:6. **And on the fifteenth day of the same month is the Feast of Unleavened Bread to the Lord; seven days you must eat unleavened bread.** 7. **In the first day you shall have a holy gathering; you shall do no labor in it.** 8. **But you shall offer an offering made by fire to the Lord seven days; in the seventh day is a holy gathering; you shall do no labor in it.** This command to do no work is different from the command in Exodus 20:8-10, in which we are told not to do any manner of work. See the explanation on page 3 under Sabbath.

The second day is the Libation, which refers to pouring water from the Pool of Shilokh (Siloam) on the altar. Water from this pool was used with the ashes of the red heifer. Rabbis point out that each kind of vegetation in the Lulav requires a lot of water.

During the time spent in the booth, each family has spiritual guests as well as earthly guests. These spiritual guests include Abraham, Isaac, Jacob, Joseph, Sarah, Rebecca, Leah, Rachel, Miriam, Hannah, Esther, Moses, Aaron, David, and others. Each family member contributes to the "conversations" with the guests. Neighbors, other friends, relatives, and the poor are expected to drop in, some bringing a dish to share as the spirit leads. Each family visits other families.

Days from the third day through the sixth day are called Ushpizin (from an Aramaic word meaning guests), calling for a great deal of visiting and the invitation of many spiritual and earthly visitors, especially the poor, who cannot repay. This feeding the poor is in line with the admonition of Jesus in Luke 14:12. **And He was saying even to the one who invited Him, When you would make a breakfast or supper, call neither your friends nor your brothers nor your kin nor rich**

neighbors, lest they would *also* invite you and it would be repayment to you. 13. **But when you would make a banquet you must always invite poor, crippled, lame, blind:** 14. **then you will be blessed, because they do not have *the means* to repay you, for it will be repaid to you in the resurrection of the righteous.**

On the third day, Ecclesiastes is read as a reminder of human frailties, a follow-up of Yom Kippur.

The sixth day is a cry for salvation, "Hoshea na rabah" "Save us now! Let us increase!" This is a time for repentance, necessary for salvation, and a reminder of Yom Kippur. On this day during the second temple period (Jesus' day), there was a procession through the streets of Jerusalem, singing Hoshea na! from Psalm 118:25. Hoshea na, written in Greek as Hosanna, means Save us! Now!! Some might say that this could have been the date of Jesus' triumphal entry, but the date is not what is most important. The critical point is that all those at Jesus' triumphal entry knew about this practice and the full meaning of it.

The seventh day is another partial Sabbath, called Shemini Atseret (Conclusion). This is celebrated back in the house. On this day the children pray, thanking God for a good harvest, praying for rain for the coming year for another good harvest. John 7:37. **And on the final Sabbath day of the feast Jesus stood and cried out saying, If anyone would drink he must continually come to Me and he must continually drink. 38. The one who believes in Me, just as the Scripture said, rivers of living water will flow out from his inner being. 39. And He said this about the Spirit, which those who believe in Him were about to take: for *the* Spirit was not yet *given*, because Jesus was not yet glorified.** Other Scriptures attesting this are Proverbs 18:4. **The words of a man's mouth are like deep waters, and the fountain of wisdom like a flowing brook.**, and Isaiah 58:11. **And the Lord shall guide you continually, and satisfy your soul in drought, and make strong your bones; and you shall be like a watered garden, and like a spring of water, whose**

waters fail not. Living water is a symbol of Torah, the Word of God.

The eighth day is a post-Biblical holiday called Simchat Torah, Joy of the Torah, which in Jerusalem is combined with Shemini Atseret (Conclusion). Simchat Torah is the most joyful day of the year when the annual reading through of the Torah is completed (Deuteronomy 34:5-12) and the reading for the coming year is begun (Genesis 1:1-31). The first verses of Genesis are read immediately following the reading of the last verses of Deuteronomy to provide continuity, so there will not be a time that Torah reading is completed.

The symbolism here is of marriage, with the synagogue reader called bride or groom. There are two readers, with one reading the Deuteronomy passage, the other the Genesis. During the Genesis reading the congregation chants "And there was evening and there was morning, one day." They repeat that for the "second day" "third day," etc. They also read Joshua 1:1-18. 1. **And it was after the death of Moses the servant of the Lord that the Lord spoke to Joshua the son of**

Nun, Moses' minister, saying, 2. Moses my servant
is dead; now therefore arise, cross over the Jordan,
you, and all this people, to the land which I give to
them, to the people of Israel. 3. Every place that the
sole of your foot shall tread upon, that I have given
to you, as I said to Moses. 4. From the wilderness
and this Lebanon to the great river, the river
Euphrates, all the land of the Hittites, and to the
Great Sea toward the going down of the sun, shall
be your border. 5. No man shall be able to stand
before you all the days of your life; as I was with
Moses, so I will be with you; I will not fail you, nor
forsake you. 6. Be strong and courageous; for you
shall cause this people to inherit the land, which I
swore to their fathers to give them. 7. Only be
strong and very courageous, that you may observe
to do according to all the Torah, which Moses my
servant commanded you; turn not from it to the right
hand or to the left, that you may prosper wherever
you go. 8. This Book of the Torah shall not depart
from your mouth; but you shall meditate on it day

and night, that you may observe to do according to all that is written on it; for then you shall make your way prosperous, and then you shall have good success. 9. Have I not commanded you? Be strong and courageous; be not afraid, nor be dismayed; for the Lord your God is with you wherever you go. 10. Then Joshua commanded the officers of the people, saying, 11. Pass through the camp, and command the people, saying, Prepare provisions; for within three days you shall cross over this Jordan, to go in to possess the land, which the Lord your God gives you to possess. 12. And to the Reubenites, and to the Gadites, and to the half tribe of Manasseh, spoke Joshua, saying, 13. Remember the word which Moses the servant of the Lord commanded you, saying, The Lord your God has given you rest, and has given you this land. 14. Your wives, your little ones, and your cattle, shall remain in the land which Moses gave you on this side of the Jordan; but you shall pass armed before your brothers, all the mighty men of valor, and help them; 15. When the

Lord should give your brothers rest, as he has given you, and when they also shall possess the land which the Lord your God gives them; then you shall return to the land of your possession, and enjoy it, which Moses the Lord's servant gave you on this side of the Jordan toward the sunrise. 16. And they answered Joshua, saying, All that you command us we will do, and wherever you send us, we will go. 17. As we listened to Moses in all things, so will we listen to you; only the Lord your God be with you, as he was with Moses. 18. If any rebels against your commandment, and will not listen to your words in all that you command him, he shall be put to death; only be strong and courageous.

This concludes the *appointed* seasons from Leviticus 23, but there is one more major Jewish holiday, reported in the Gospel of John.

Hanukkah

Hebrew Name: Hanukkah, meaning Dedication. Although normally spelled Hanukkah in English, the correct spelling would be Khanukkah.

Scripture Reference: John 10:22. There is no Reference in Leviticus. Date: 25 Kislev, late November to late December.

Symbolized by a Hanukkah menorah, called Hanukkiah, with eight candles, plus a shamash, which is a ninth candle used to light the other candles.

Jesus celebrated Hanukkah, so we should know something about it.

The history of Hanukkah began with the Hellenist movement in Judaism. This movement started in 332BC when Alexander the Great overran Israel on his way from Syria to Egypt. Unlike other ancient conquerors that forced their captives to accept the religion of the conqueror, Alexander let each nation he conquered continue to worship as it pleased. In Israel life was good, as Alexander's leaders who were brought in to oversee governing and to promote business, brought prosperity with them. But they also brought the Greek theater, games, and gymnasiums. The introduction of this foreign culture into the main-stream of Jewish life in Jerusalem led many of the elite, in both business and the temple, the ruling class, to go to the theater or games instead of to a synagogue. These elite, who treasured Greek culture, were called Hellenists.

After the death of Alexander the Great (323 BC), his empire was divided among his generals. Judea and Egypt were ruled by Ptolemy, Syria by Seleucus, Greece by Antigonus.

As the years went on the Hellenists became more and more Greek, even speaking Greek instead of Hebrew. The freedom to travel that came with the expanse, security, and wealth from Greek control of the civilized world had Jewish businessmen moving to various parts of the empire. In 250BC, the king of Egypt, Ptolmey Philadelphus, brought 70 men, seven from each of the ten tribes, to Alexandria Egypt to translate the Hebrew Scriptures into Greek. Since they were from the ten tribes there would not have been one scribe among them. Their translation is called the Septuagint, the Latin word for seventy, and the number of men who did the translating.

In the eyes of the Jewish purists, this foreign culture was contradictory to Judaism. Judaism says, "What is good is beautiful," while Greek culture says "What is beautiful is good."

In the year 198 BC, Judea fell to the armies of Antiochus III, the Greek king of Assyria, who granted the

Jews many privileges, including religious rights. Twenty-three years later, in 175 BC, a new king ruled over Assyria, Antiochus Epiphanes (the Illustrious).

The Hellenists continued to become more and more Greek. They had built a gymnasium in Jerusalem, which they attended more frequently than the Temple. They had their Holy Torah in Greek (the infamous Septuagint – a bad and incorrect translation) and ceased to study and speak Hebrew; some of the men even underwent operations to reverse their "sign of the covenant in the flesh" — the circumcision!

In a reversal of previous policy by the Greek leaders this king decreed that no one in any part of his kingdom could worship any god but the Greek gods. He forced everyone in his kingdom to worship the Greek gods. Thus, with the Jewish Hellenists leading the parade, God's Temple in Jerusalem was turned into a shrine of the Greek gods, and the pious Jews had to leave town or accept these strange gods.

In the village of Modin, in the Hills of Judea, less than

twenty-five miles from Jerusalem, the Greek soldiers encountered resistance: The aged high priest, Mattathias the Hasmonaean, not only refused to lead the people of his village in the forbidden sacrifice — but when a Hellenist Jew did offer a sacrifice, he drew a sword and slaughtered the man. His five sons came to his aid, killing the soldiers of the small Greek detachment that came into the village to carry the Hellenization process.

This unprecedented act of religious zeal raised the banner of revolt. Mattathias' rallying call is very important to note (and to remember): Mi L'Adona'y Ela'y — whosoever is for God, let him come to me! This battle cry, and the men who heeded its message, were a 'first' in the annals of human history: a totally volunteer army established to wage war not for gain of territory nor for booty — but merely for the right to do something (worship) as they wished.

In other words, the battle was for a principle, for an ideal! It is on this precedence that all future noble causes would be fought. Mattathias, in this respect is the true father of American democracy – the first, the originator of the principle upon which stands the Declaration of Independence! The first fighter for human rights!

In the year 166 B.C.E. Mattathias died (of old age, it is believed). Many pious Jews who fled Hellenistic persecution in Jerusalem and other towns and hamlets had by then joined his followers from Modin. His third son, Yehuda (Judah), led them as they began to nibble at the Greek armies – attacking by surprise here and there, choosing the time and place of battle that would give them the advantage over their numerically superior and better equipped enemy.

Judah adopted as his motto the words from the book of Exodus: Mi Camokha Ba'Elim Adona'y (Exodus 15:11) – who is like unto Thee, Oh Lord, among the mighty. The initials of the Hebrew words spelled Maccabee – a name by which first Judah and later his army became known. (It was not until much later, with *the help of a misspelling of the Hebrew word maccabee that the meaning hammer, a nickname for the Hasmoneans, came into existence!)*

Judah turned out to be a great military strategist. In quick succession, he defeated the legions of the Greek generals Apollonius, Seron, Gorgias and Lysias. With the defeat of Lysias the road to the capital, Jerusalem, was open, and the city lay undefended.

Judah and his men entered David's capital, driving before them the host of Hellenized Jews who realized that Jerusalem would no longer be a haven for them. Then the Maccabees cleansed the Temple, kindled the eternal light and offered thanksgiving sacrifices. This section in italics is copied from "Basic Judaism" written by Rabbi Eliezer Ben-Yehuda.

The Hellenists, who had been the ones to forsake the synagogue, the Jewish practices, and the Hebrew language, called themselves Tsadeek, meaning Righteous. They called those who remained true to God and Judaism as Lifrot, meaning Broke Away, and

Hasidim, meaning Pious. They were also called Parush, meaning self-denying, dissident, seceder, seclusive, sanctimonious. Tsadeek is written in Greek as Sadducee, while Parush is written as Pharisee.

The Hellenists are seen in Acts 6:1, 9:29, and 11:20.

6.1. And in those days as the disciples were increasing *in number* there was a complaint of the Hellenists against the Hebrews, because their widows were being neglected in the daily service.

9: 29. and he was speaking and debating with the Hellenists, and they were trying to kill him.

11:20. But some of them were men of Cyprus and Cyrene, who when they came into Antioch were speaking then to the Hellenists preaching the Good News of the Lord Jesus.

The word "Hanukkah" means dedication, recalling the reconsecration of the Temple to the worship of God, which took place on the 25th of Kislev in the year 164

BC. The duration of the holiday, eight days, is based on the process of purification, which takes eight days.

Tradition tells of the miracle of the oil: a small vessel of pure oil (oil that had been prepared by the priests in the prescribed manner) was all that the Maccabees found in the Temple. It would have taken eight days to prepare new oil, and they were sure the oil they had found would not serve the Eternal Light for more than one day. The Eternal Light's flame was a symbol of the establishment of "normal" conditions of Jewish worship in the Temple. The Maccabees were in a dilemma: Should they wait till the new oil was ready? The people were anxious to begin worship in the Temple again; or should they kindle the flame, and allow it to go out when the oil was gone? The Maccabees made a choice — for the immediate service of God. They kindled the light, and it continued to burn until the new oil was ready (which is to say, for eight days). Thus those celebrating Hanukkah kindle lights for eight days, and we[1] have

---

[1] "We" is the appropriate pronoun since this was written by Rabbi BenYehuda for his synagogue use.

given the holiday a second name, "Hag Ha'urim" — the Festival of Lights.

Immediately after the restoration of the Temple, Judah and his brothers turned over the reigns of leadership to the priests and Levites in the Temple. They retired from public office and went back to the little village of Modin, only to be called back when the Greek armies returned.

One by one the Maccabee brothers fell in the battle to keep Judaea Jewish — until only one, Simon, remained alive. By then, 142 B.C.E., the Antioch government was involved in battle with the Parthian Empire and had internal troubles in Asia Minor, and so a treaty was signed between Antioch and Judaea allowing the Jews self-government. The Jews in Jerusalem wanted to crown Simon king, but he refused, claiming that only descendants of David had a right to the crown of Jerusalem; when the people still insisted that he remain as their leader, he accepted the title "Nassi" — president — not king.

The Hebrew for lamp is "menorah." On Hanukkah, though, there is a special menorah, called "Hanukkiyah." The difference between a regular "Jewish" menorah and a hanukkiyah is that the former has seven branches and the latter has nine. The "ninth" candle is the "Shamash" (sexton), which is lit first, without a blessing, with which the other candles are lit. With the Shamash we kindle one light on the first night, and an additional light every succeeding night, so that on the last night all eight candles are lit. These paragraphs in italics are copied from "Basic Judaism" by Rabbi Eliezer Ben-Yehuda.

The hanukkiyah is the symbol next to the heading of this section, with the center Shamash and the candle for the first night lighted. The candles for each evening are always lighted from right to left.

Hanukkah, celebrating victory over repression and the freedom to worship their own religion, is comparable to the Fourth of July in the US. Hanukkah is the victory of Godliness over heathenism, with today's parallel of Godliness vs. Humanism, as Humanism honors the same values that Hellenism did two thousand years ago. Our public schools permit the teaching of paganism, the occult, witchcraft, and the acceptability of homosexuality and abortion, while they deny the teaching of the Judeo-Christian principles on which this nation was founded.

Let's bring the celebration of Hanukkah back into the Church.

For the Church:

The Feast of Booths completes the annual agricultural cycle. It is a time to remember all that the Lord has brought us through, individually and collectively. The traditions that make this mean so much are not to be copied from Judaism en masse, but we are to seek the spiritual meanings and keep them in some form. We do need to pay attention to the Scriptural commands, to make booths, to remember the bondage that we have left behind, to remember the poor, who are still in the bondage of poverty. The spiritual guests in the home are to remain, to visit throughout the year. The time to feed, bless, love the poor is not to be forgotten until the next Feast of Booths, but is to be a part of our way of life. Romans 12:8. **or the one who encourages in encouragement: the one who shares, in sincerity** *without grudging,* **the protector or guardian giving aid in diligent eagerness, the one who is merciful in cheerfulness.** This is also a time for family.

This is a time to look for the Messianic reign, to prepare the bride and the wedding feast. Revelation 19:5. **And a voice came out from heaven saying,**

> **You, all His servants, and those who fear Him,**
> **the least and the greatest,** (Psalm 115:13)
> **must continually sing praises**
> **in honor of our God.** (Psalm 22:23, 134:1, 135:1)

6. **And I heard a sound like a great crowd and like a sound of many waters** (Ezekiel 1:24, 43:2) **and like a sound of strong thunders saying, Hallelujah, because our God the Lord of Hosts did reign.** (Exodus 15:18, Psalm 22:28, 93:1, 99:1, Daniel 7:14, Zechariah 14:9)

7. **Let us rejoice and be glad**
   and we will give Him the glory,
   because the marriage festival of the Lamb has come and His wife has prepared herself

8. **and it was given to her that she would be clothed**

priest can sacrifice an animal other than the red heifer. The Scriptures most often cited by rabbis in saying sacrifices are no longer necessary are Hosea 6:6. **For I desired loyal love, and not sacrifice; and the knowledge of God more than burnt offerings.** and 1 Samuel 15:22. **And Samuel said, Has the Lord as great delight in burnt offerings and sacrifices, as in obeying the voice of the Lord? Behold, to obey is better than sacrifice, and to listen better than the fat of rams.** A note about the statement in Hosea is significant: the NIV translates the noun as acknowledgment instead of knowledge, but knowledge is correct. Even the demons acknowledge Him, but true knowledge must be intimate, as we accept Him as our Lord and Savior, and as our Husband. God must be the center of each Christian life and each Jewish life.

The study of the Scriptures quoted in this booklet and then putting them into action reinforces the theme of this series, calling the Church to understand its Jewish roots. It is not necessary to keep all the traditions, but we do need to study the Hebrew Scriptures to pick up the factors on which the Jewish traditions are based, and do everything Scripture ordains.

Each church needs to transition carefully, phasing in appropriate celebrations and phasing out the inappropriate pagan elements. The point is to bring Christians to a better understanding of God and His commandments, returning confidently to the seasons that Jesus celebrated.

Each season commanded here is significant for every life dedicated to His service. This is the timetable Jesus, every New Testament author, all the apostles and disciples followed. The Jewish people refer to this yearly schedule as "The Rhythm of Life." The Soncino Chumash speaks of this rhythm as *"..the culmination of a process. First comes redemption (Pesach); then the purpose of redemption (receiving the Torah on Shavuot); and, finally, these lessons are brought into our everyday lives when we find our joy in observing the commandments (Sukkot). In addition, Sukkot is the culmination of the Tishrei process of repentance and*

*atonement, when we succeed in dragging ourselves out
of the morass of sin."*

We would all like to see the power of the first century
church operating in our communities and our nation. We
are not going to see the power until we match that
church in holiness, love, unity, and obedience to what
they knew as Scripture, what we irreverently call "Old
Testament." Remember Matthew 5:17, 18. **Do not think
that I came to abolish the Torah or the Prophets: I
did not come to abolish but to bring *spiritual*
abundance. 18. For truly I say to you: until the sky
and the earth would pass away, not one yod or one
vav could ever pass away from the Torah, until
everything would come to pass.** (Luke 16:17)

CONCLUSION

The history of the removal of the Jewish roots is very painful to review. It is shameful the way the Church has behaved, but this is something Christians should know.

The reason Jewish Roots were lost early in Church history is that many of our often-revered Church Fathers were anti-Semitic, deliberately changing Jewish celebrations and altering some doctrines to make a complete break from Judaism. In the second century Justin Martyr, Polycarp, and Marcion were among those beginning the onslaught against the Jewish people and Judaism. Marcion in the middle of the second century was the first to write that the New Covenant had replaced all previous covenants – and at the time he was known as a heretic. In the fourth century John Chrysostom, known for powerful, eloquent sermons, gave a series of seventeen virulently anti-Semitic sermons at a time when the pagan celebration of Ishtar, the fertility goddess, was made official to replace Passover for the celebration of Jesus' death and resurrection. Some had begun this celebration of Ishtar late in the second century. Also, the Roman winter solstice celebration in honor of the god Saturn was established as the celebration of Jesus' birth. In the fifth century Augustine brought Greek philosophy into Christian theology, which has influenced the Church to this day.

The celebrations made official in the fourth century put a seal on the separation from Judaism and set the stage for violence against the Jewish people. Jewish people even today often view Christians as "the enemy" — but with good reason. Over the centuries Christians have outperformed all other groups combined in the killing of Jews. There were numerous pogroms, brutal attacks on entire Jewish villages, throughout Europe from early on through the Holocaust.

In 1492 Ferdinand and Isabella forced all the Jews to leave Spain. Such forced exoduses were common, with Jews moving from one country to another, virtually all over Europe. Every European country expelled Jews at least once. Jews were forbidden to own land until they came to the American colonies. The Spanish Inquisition is well known for cruelty to the Jewish people, forcing conversions. Because of these and even persecution, to Jewish people crosses and crusades are among the most evil things imaginable.

The Holocaust was not the end of anti-Semitism and not the sole evidence of it in WW II. During the Holocaust not one Christian denomination spoke out against the attempted extermination of the Jewish people, nor did the major allied governments take action. Even now, in the 21st century, Anti-Semitism is very strong at the UN and is rising throughout the world, especially in Europe.

The seventh chapter of Proverbs warns against the sort of heresy that seduced the Church from its Jewish roots. This chapter speaks of a forbidden woman, a harlot, and how she entices a man into her lair. Rabbinic commentary makes the allusion to harlotry, saying, "Heresy, the harlot, bides its time and begins casually. Someone slowly goes astray, distancing himself from the Torah's moral values, until he becomes the harlot's guest. He becomes accustomed to going to her, until she controls him." (Vilna Gaon, quoted in the Artscroll Tanakh)

To understand the Jewish roots of Christianity, look first to the Hebrew Scriptures. Among the earliest things the Church did to divorce from Judaism was changing the seasons of the Lord. These seasons are essential for Christians to honor. Let each congregation now begin to recognize the Lord's Seasons and teach on our obligation to honor the same holy days that Jesus honored. Remember the words of the Lord to Joshua: **This Book of the Torah shall not depart from your mouth; but you shall meditate on it day and night, that you may observe to do according to all that is written on it; for then you shall make your way prosperous, and then you shall have good success.** (Joshua 1:8)

Unless otherwise noted, Old Testament quotes are from Soncino Tanakh, Davka, Inc. New Testament quotes are from the Power New Testament, Wm. J. Morford.

	Spring		
v. 3	v. 5	v. 6	v. 10
SHABBAT	**PASSOVER**	**UNLEAVENED BREAD**	**FIRST FRUITS**
Sabbath			
1. Every seventh day is for rest and time with the Lord.	1. Deliverance from Egyptian bondage.	1. Seven days of remembering deliverance from Egyptian bondage. 2. Unleavened bread represents sinlessness. 3. Resurrection.	1. Offering of the barley harvest, the 1st of the First Fruits, the second day of Unleavened Bread.
Added by the NT:	2. Memory of Jesus' atoning sacrifice, by His death. 3. Deliverance from spiritual bondage.	4. The Bread of John 6:22-59.	2. Jesus' resurrection.

AS
1. For
   aft
   Fru
   cele
   Jes
   asc

NOTE: THE DAY OF MEMORIAL is commonly called Rosh Hashanah, ℕ
blowing of Trumpets..." From this it has been named the Feast of Trumpets
Succot are the Seasons that are called Feasts in Leviticus 23. These plus Sha⋁

Late Spring v. 15 **SHAVUOT** Pentecost	Fall v. 24 **DAY OF** **MEMORIAL**	v. 27 **YOM** **KIPPUR**	v. 34 **SUCCOT** Tabernacles
1. Offering of the wheat harvest, the 2nd First Fruits. 2. Anniversary of the giving of Torah	1. A day for remembering everything the Lord has done for us, individually & collectively. 2. A call to repentance, by the shofar. 3. Anniversary of creation. 4. Judgment Day.	1. A day of total fasting for repentance. 2. This calls for a determination to do better than you did last year, to truly love your neighbor.	1. The eight day feast of joy for the fall harvest, the 3rd First Fruits. 2. This is when trumpets are blown. 3. Eighth day is Shemini Atseret, (conclusion).

)N

3. Celebration
   of the baptism
   of the Holy
   Spirit.

4. The
   Wedding
   Supper.

r, by the Jewish people. In the KJV it was translated "..a Memorial of the
ough it is not a feast and a trumpet is not called for. Unleavened Bread and
called feasts in Exodus 23 & 34. Shabbat is called a feast in Exodus 13:6.

in brilliant pure fine linen: for the fine linen is the righteous deeds of the saints. (Isaiah 61:10)

Then he said to me, You must now write: Blessed are those who have been called to the wedding supper of the Lamb. And he said to me, These are the true words of God. (Revelation 19:9)

37. These are the appointed festivals of the Lord, which you shall proclaim to be holy gatherings, to offer an offering made by fire to the Lord, a burnt offering, and a meal offering, a sacrifice, and drink offerings, every thing upon his day; :38. Beside the Sabbaths of the Lord, and beside your gifts, and beside all your vows, and beside all your freewill offerings, which you give to the Lord. 39. Also in the fifteenth day of the seventh month, when you have gathered in the fruit of the land, you shall keep a feast to the Lord seven days; on the first day shall be a Sabbath, and on the eighth day shall be a Sabbath. 40. And you shall take on the first day the boughs of goodly trees, branches of palm trees, and the boughs of thick trees, and willows of the brook;

and you shall rejoice before the Lord your God seven days. 41. **And you shall keep it a feast to the Lord seven days in the year. It shall be a statute forever in your generations; you shall celebrate it in the seventh month.** 42. **You shall dwell in booths seven days; all who are Israelites born shall dwell in booths;** 43. **That your generations may know that I made the people of Israel to dwell in booths, when I brought them out of the land of Egypt; I am the Lord your God.** 44. **And Moses declared to the people of Israel the feasts of the Lord.** (Leviticus 23:37-44)

The offerings mentioned for these feasts include animal sacrifices, which no Christian would make. The Jewish people have not offered animal sacrifices since the temple was destroyed in 70 AD because the sacrifices can only be offered in one place – on Mount Moriah in Jerusalem. Even now, nearly 2,000 years after the destruction of the temple, the temple mount is still in the hands of heathens, since the Mosque of Omar stands directly over the rock where Abraham offered Isaac, which is the only place in the world that a Jewish